Exotic animal carers must do special training so they know how to care for the special needs of these animals.

Let's see what a working day is like for three different exotic animal carers.

This exotic animal carer looks after tigers.

THE SNAKE HANDLER

Imagine being a snake handler. Sounds dangerous! But snake handlers know all about snakes and other **reptiles**. Most snake handlers work at zoos.

Here's a snake handler with one of the largest snakes in the world – a python.

There are about 6000 different kinds of reptiles in the world. Snakes, tortoises, lizards and crocodiles are all reptiles.

Meet Some Snake Friends

Snake handlers look after many kinds of snakes, such as cobras, pythons and tree snakes.

King cobras are very **venomous**. One bite could kill a snake handler. So a snake handler must be very careful when holding this snake.

King cobras are from Asia or south-east Asia.

Pythons wrap themselves around their **prey**. They squeeze the animal so it can't breathe any more. Then pythons swallow their prey whole!

African tree snakes are small and shy and not dangerous to people. They come out at night to eat lizards and tree frogs.

African tree snakes hide during the day.

Snake Homes

Snake handlers look after the snake cages. The cages are built to be like the snake's home in the wild.

Cobras like lots of leaves to hide under. Pythons like thick grass and rocks to rub against. All snakes like to curl up inside hollow logs.

Keeping Warm and Cosy

Snakes are **cold-blooded**. This means they can't make their own heat to warm their bodies. In the wild, snakes get warm by lying in the sun or on warm rocks.

In a zoo, the snake handler makes sure the snakes keep warm by heating their cages with special heat lights.

Snakes stretch out to warm their bodies. Then they curl up quickly to stay warm.

Cleaning Up

Snake handlers also have to clean the snake cages. This can be tricky. First, they need to move the snake! They put the snake in another cage or in a large bucket.

Now for the gross part! The snake handler picks up all the rotten leaves and snake poo in the cage.

The snake handler uses a long hook to pick up this rattlesnake gently.

What's for Lunch?

Another job is feeding the snakes. In the wild, snakes eat mice, rats, chicks, lizards and even other snakes. So, they need to eat the same food as they would eat in the wild.

Snakes don't chew their food. They eat it whole. The pictures below show an anaconda eating a large rodent.

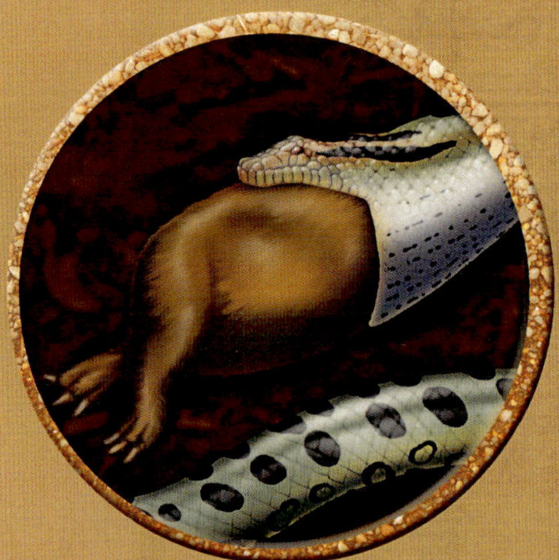

The snake opens its mouth very, very wide.

It swallows its food whole.

An anaconda is one of the biggest snakes in the world. It can sometimes last on one meal for a year! But it has to be a very big meal such as a deer, large rodent or a pig.

This viper snake is eating a mouse.

A bump can be seen moving down the snake's body, from its mouth to its stomach.

The food is broken down in the snake's stomach.

How would you like to look after baby orang-utans? That's what orang-utan carers do at this Malaysian wildlife park. Some baby orang-utans in the wildlife park are only a few weeks old. They need lots of cuddles!

The word "orang-utan" means "man of the forest" in the Malay language.

The Great Apes

Orang-utans, gorillas and chimpanzees are all great **apes**.

Where's Mum?

All the orang-utans at this wildlife park are orphans. This means they've lost their mothers. When people cut down **rainforests**, orang-utans lose their homes.

Many rainforest trees are cut down for farming.

The babies lose their mothers. Sometimes, the baby orang-utans are hurt.

A wildlife worker cares for a baby orang-utan at the wildlife park.

A Vet Check

When a baby orang-utan arrives at the wildlife park, a **vet** checks it. The vet checks for any illnesses that could be passed to other animals.

The vet checks that the baby orang-utan is healthy.

This baby orang-utan will join other orang-utans when it is well.

At the park, there is an animal hospital. There is also a special room where the animals stay by themselves until they are well again. They can then join the other orang-utans.

Indoor and Outdoor Nursery

Looking after baby orang-utans is a twenty-four-hour job. Babies sleep and play in a **nursery** until they are four years old.

Like human babies, they cry for milk day and night. The carers feed them lots of bottles of milk.

Forest School

When the orang-utans are old enough, they go to "forest school". They learn to:

- pick fruit
- climb trees
- make a nest with leaves.

Carers teach baby orang-utans the things that wild orang-utans learn from their mums!

Going Home

Slowly, the orang-utans learn to do things by themselves. When the carers think they are ready, they let the orang-utans go back into the forest where they can live without help.

Saying goodbye is sad but the forest is the orang-utan's real home.

THE WHALE RESCUER

Whale rescuers work in a group. They look after whales that get sick or injured.

Whales can get injured if they get caught up in fishing nets.

Sometimes, whales end up on the beach. Whales are so big and heavy that they can't move back out to the sea by themselves. So the whale rescue group tries to help them.

A Day in the Life of a Whale Rescuer

Whale rescue groups get reports when a whale is injured at sea or on land. Then, they rush to the whale to try and help it.

Divers help a whale caught in a net.

If a whale is caught in a fishing net, people from the group will put on their scuba gear and jump into the sea. They will then cut the nets to free the whale.

Saving Whales on the Beach

Sometimes, a whale gets stuck on the beach. This can happen by accident if a whale gets too close to the shore and can't swim back out to sea.

A vet from the whale rescue group checks the health of the whales. Whale rescuers pour water on the whales to make sure they stay wet and cold. Then the group use special equipment to move the whales back out to sea.

This whale is being picked up in a sling and will be taken back out to sea.

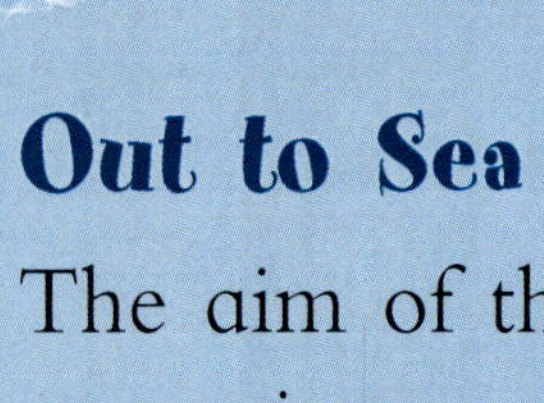

Out to Sea

The aim of the whale rescue group is to make sure a whale is free and healthy.

Whales breathe out of blowholes on top of their heads. Whales can stay under water for a long time, about twenty minutes, but they do need to rise above the water to breathe.

BECOMING AN EXOTIC ANIMAL CARER

Maybe you will become an exotic animal carer one day.

Here's how to start:

- Volunteer at a zoo.
- Join a wildlife rescue group.
- You can also study to be an animal scientist.

Feeding a hippopotamus

EXOTIC ANIMAL QUIZ

See if you can answer these questions about exotic animals.

1. Snakes in the wild keep warm by:

a. lying in the sun

b. putting on a coat

c. lying in the rain

2. A whale breathes through its:

a. nose

b. fin

c. blowhole

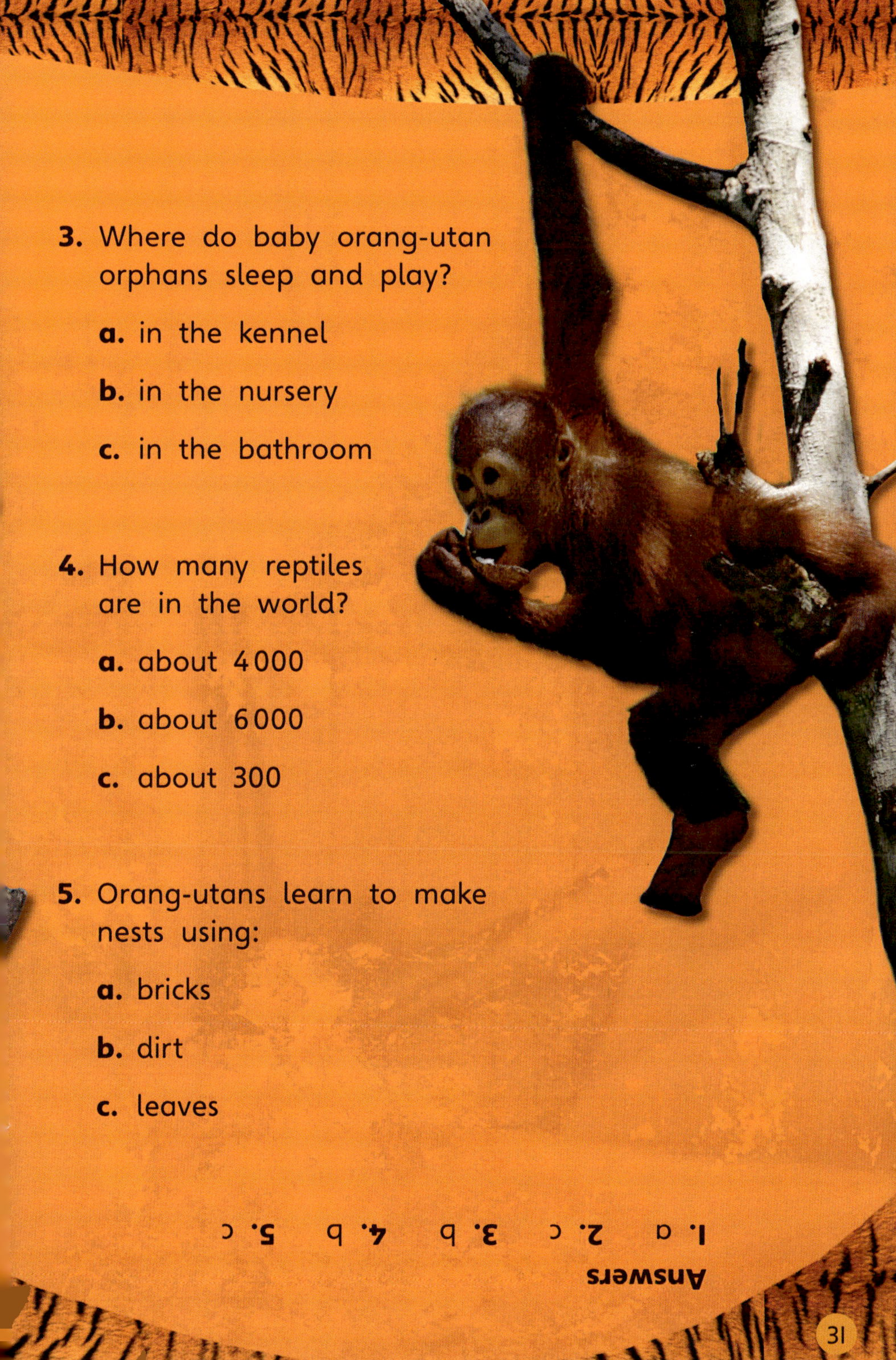

3. Where do baby orang-utan orphans sleep and play?

a. in the kennel

b. in the nursery

c. in the bathroom

4. How many reptiles are in the world?

a. about 4000

b. about 6000

c. about 300

5. Orang-utans learn to make nests using:

a. bricks

b. dirt

c. leaves

Answers

1. a **2.** c **3.** b **4.** b **5.** c

GLOSSARY

apes	animals like orang-utans, chimpanzees and gorillas that are related to humans and monkeys, but have no tail
cold-blooded	an animal whose blood changes temperature according to the environment
exotic	from another country
nursery	a room where babies sleep and play
prey	an animal killed by another animal for food
rainforests	forests with a high amount of rainfall
rare	not very common
reptiles	cold-blooded animals, such as tortoises, snakes, or crocodiles that have an outer covering of scales or plates and lay eggs
venomous	injects poison by biting
vet	an animal doctor